Rambee Boo
Practices healthy habits too!
COLORING BOOK

Copyright © 2021 WAMAN BOOKS PUBLISHING, LLC

All rights reserved. No part of this publication may be used or reproduced in any manner whatsoever without written permission of the publisher.

———— WB ————
WAMAN BOOKS

Published by:
WAMAN BOOKS PUBLISHING, LLC
WWW.WAMANBOOKS.COM

Rambee Boo & Sock

COUNT WITH RAMBEE BOO
How many bees can you count?

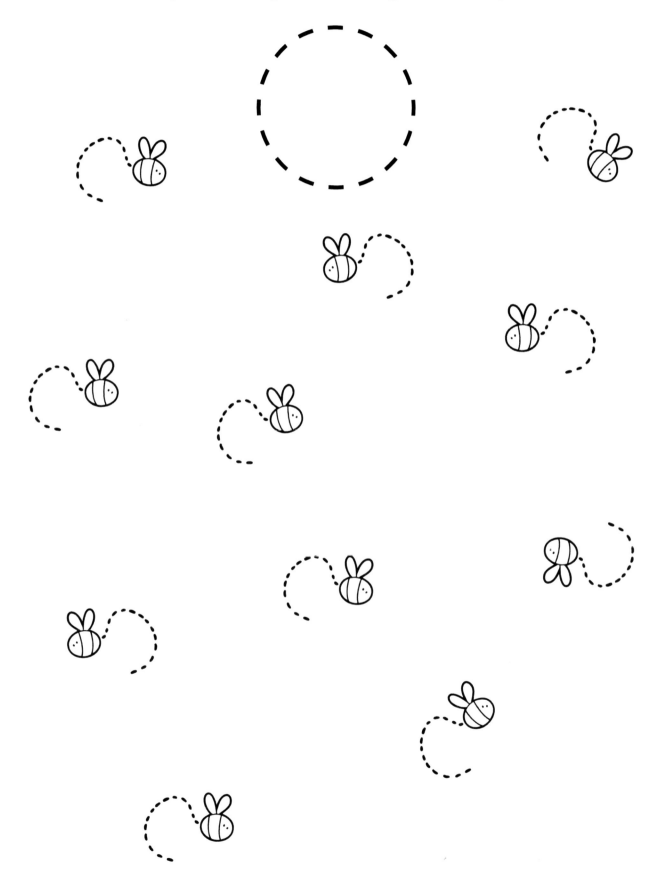

Rock and Rambee Boo love to play outside and stay ACTIVE.

CONNECT THE DOTS

Fastening your seatbelt is a good habit. Help Rock put his seatbelt on, then color the picture.

What color would you make your sock?

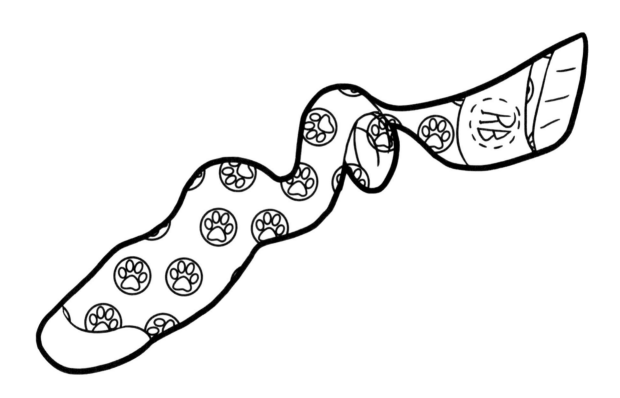

DRAW IT

Draw a picture of things you can do to stay active.

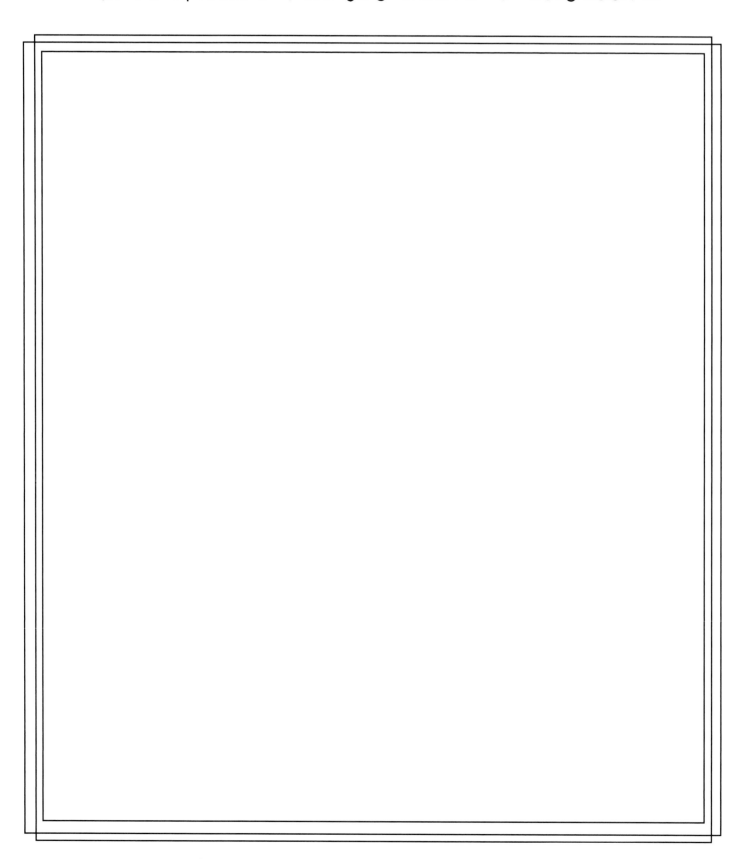

Rock loves his rain boots!

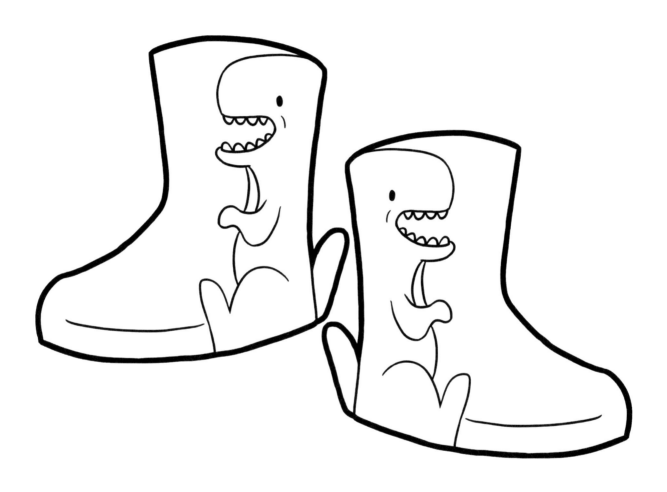

MIX & MATCH
Match the pictures of healthy snacks.

Did you know SHARING is CARING?
Rock SHARES his umbrella with Rambee Boo.

THINK OUTSIDE THE BOX

This is not an umbrella. Finish the picture.

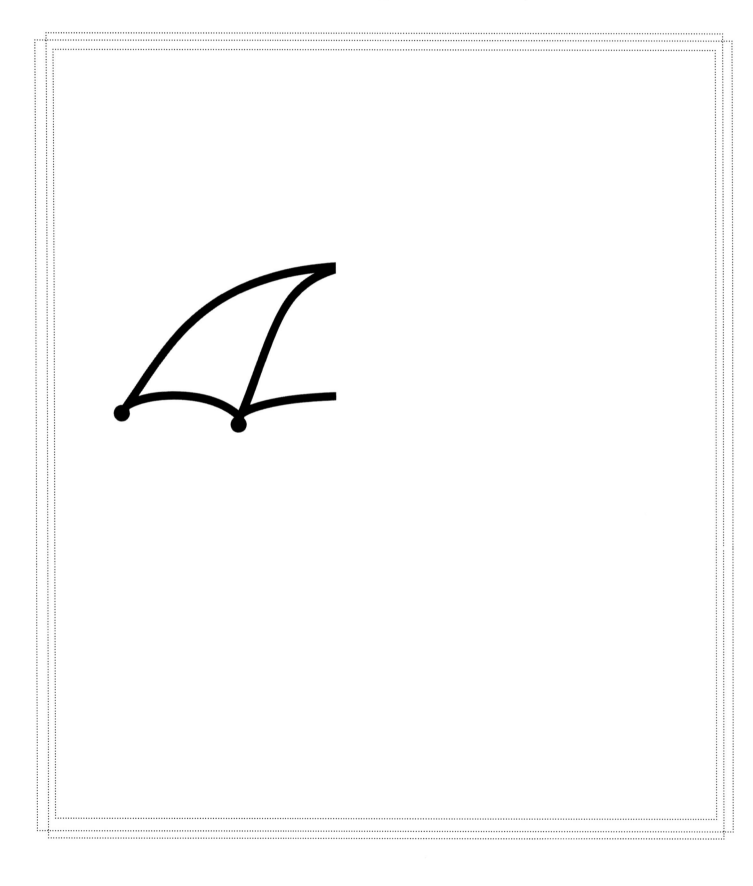

Rock and Rambee Boo HELP Mom carry groceries.

UNSCRAMBLE THE WORD

Can you figure out what the following words are?

ABERME OBO

KSCO & COKR

ELHAHTY NKSAC

EDRA MORE BKOOS

RSBUH ORYU EETHT

Rambee Boo picks flowers for Mom.

WORD MIX UP

How many words can you make using the letters from the word

RAMBEE BOO?

Rock and Rambee Boo love Mom.

WORD SEARCH

Find and circle the words from the list.

P	S	A	H	E	A	L	T	H	Y	S	N	A	C	K	S	R	D
Y	E	L	U	A	C	T	I	V	I	T	Y	N	P	R	C	E	X
M	A	N	N	E	R	S	U	P	R	Q	J	E	C	W	L	A	T
R	B	D	J	K	K	H	G	E	X	C	U	S	E	M	E	D	T
Z	H	E	A	L	T	H	Y	H	A	B	I	T	S	P	A	I	H
P	L	A	Y	R	A	M	B	E	E	B	O	O	S	R	N	N	E
K	R	E	S	P	O	N	S	I	B	I	L	I	T	Y	U	G	L
R	S	L	E	E	P	U	G	P	I	S	O	C	K	Y	P	J	M
W	O	D	S	R	L	J	E	X	E	R	C	I	S	E	Q	Z	E
X	G	C	R	W	A	S	H	I	N	G	H	A	N	D	S	Z	T
K	E	W	K	O	F	K	J	D	T	C	A	R	S	E	A	T	W
W	D	B	F	B	R	U	S	H	I	N	G	T	E	E	T	H	N

Activity
Brushing teeth
Carseat
Clean up
Excuse me
Exercise healthy habits
Healthy Snacks
Helmet
Manners

Play
Rambee Boo
Reading
Responsibility
Rock
Sleep
Sock
Washing hands

Rock COMFORTS Rambee Boo when he's sad.

CONNECT THE DOTS

Getting enough sleep is very important for your body and a HEALTHY habit! Help make a cozy bed for Rambee Boo by connecting the dots then color the picture.

Did you know that it's important to EXERCISE?
Rock takes Rambee Boo for a WALK every day.

COUNT WITH RAMBEE BOO
How many bones can you count?

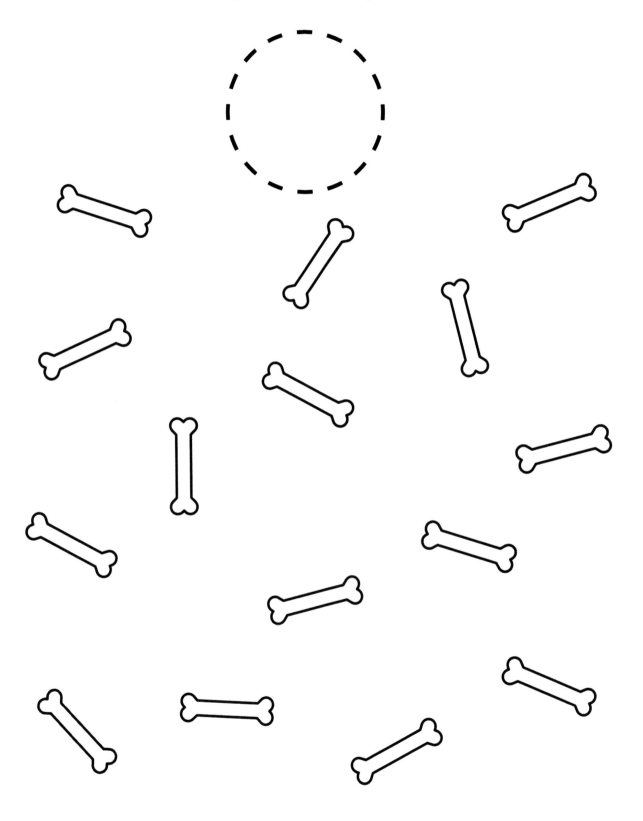

Did you know that PLAYING OUTSIDE, getting FRESH AIR and EXERCISING, helps your body to be healthy?

DRAW IT

Draw a picture of healthy snacks you like to eat.

Rock plays baseball outside to stay ACTIVE.

MIX & MATCH
Match the pictures of ways to STAY HEALTHY.

Rock stays safe by wearing his HELMET when he's riding his bike.

THINK OUTSIDE THE BOX

This is not a tree. Finish the picture.

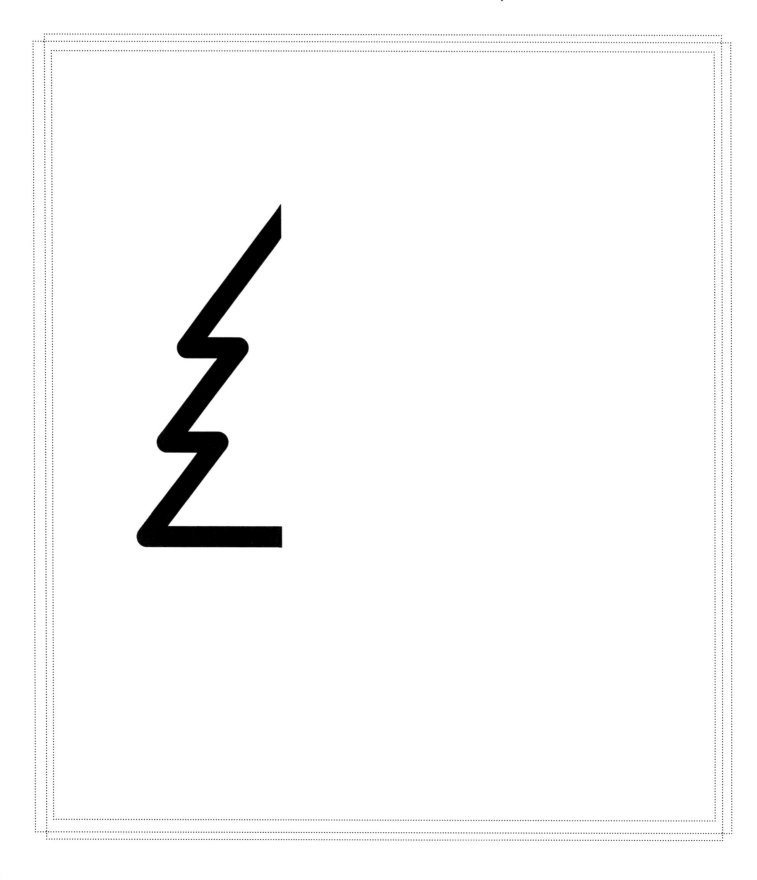

Remember to BUCKLE UP and stay in your CAR SEAT so you can be SAFE when you're in the car.

UNSCRAMBLE THE WORD

Can you figure out what the following words are?

SWHA UORY ANHDS

SECRXEIE

TAYS TACVEI

SOWH KSDNEINS

PEHL LEACN PU

Rock and Rambee Boo make Mom a card for Mother's Day to show her how much they CARE.

WORD MIX UP

How many words can you make using the letters from the word

RAMBEE AND ROCK ?

Rock HELPS out on laundry day by putting away his clothes.

WORD SEARCH

Find and circle the words from the list.

A	N	L	M	T	Z	Q	B	O	J	C	C	A	X	B	G	H	G
V	O	G	P	Q	O	B	A	C	C	H	P	P	H	B	R	K	R
Y	E	R	A	E	P	M	N	E	A	E	M	P	U	R	A	I	O
O	W	G	N	P	A	S	A	M	R	E	E	L	M	O	P	D	N
G	R	A	E	C	P	S	N	T	R	S	F	E	M	C	E	M	O
U	K	A	T	T	E	L	A	Q	O	E	R	S	U	C	S	F	L
R	B	O	N	E	A	L	E	Z	T	S	Z	A	S	O	M	R	A
T	O	E	J	G	R	B	E	S	S	T	C	U	U	L	I	U	B
W	W	E	A	H	E	E	L	R	L	I	H	C	Z	I	L	I	A
S	J	U	V	S	H	S	E	E	Y	C	P	E	T	W	K	T	R
C	R	A	C	K	E	R	S	N	S	K	S	K	M	V	P	A	S
L	O	C	P	R	E	T	Z	E	L	S	S	V	F	W	J	O	Z

Apples
Applesauce
Banana
Broccoli
Carrots
Celery
Cheese Stick
Crackers
Fruit
Grapes

Granola bars
Hummus
Milk
Oranges
Peas
Pretzels
Tomato
Vegetables
Water
Yogurt

Rock enjoys playing on his device.
He uses a timer to remind himself when it's time to get off.

CONNECT THE DOTS

Reading is a very good habit. Can you make a new book for Rock to read? Design a cover and add a title.

Rock remembers to use good MANNERS by saying THANK YOU to Rambee Boo!

COUNT WITH RAMBEE BOO

How many socks can you count?

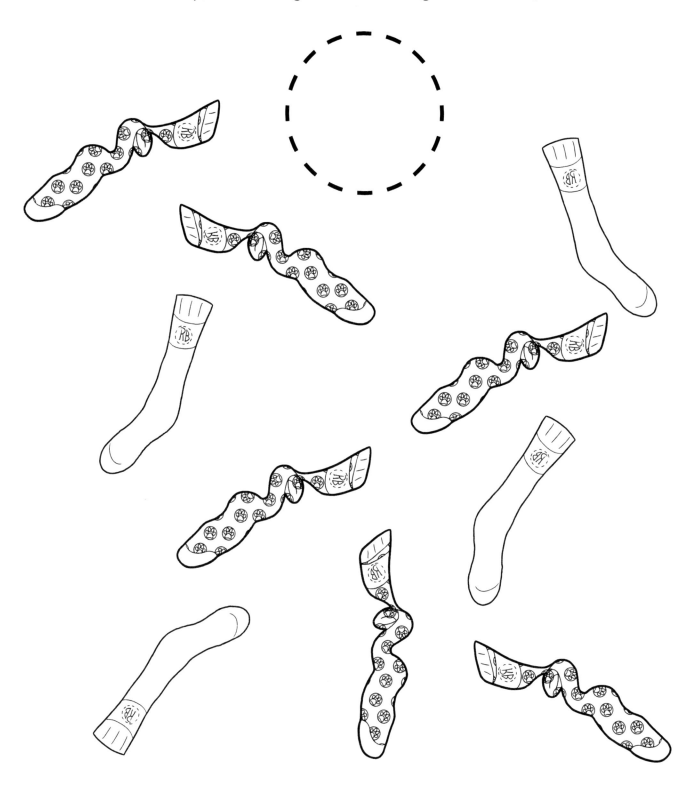

Rock always SNEEZES into his elbow so he doesn't SPREAD GERMS! Silly Rambee Boo...he blew his tissue!

DRAW IT

Draw a picture of an act of kindness.

Good hygiene – WASHING YOUR HANDS is a very HEALTHY HABIT. You should wash your hands when you come in from being outside, before you eat, after you sneeze, after you go potty and after you blow your nose.

MIX & MATCH
Match the pictures of Rambee Boo.

Rock and Rambee Boo love eating yummy VEGETABLES because they are a healthy food choice.

THINK OUTSIDE THE BOX

This is not a snowman. Finish the picture.

Did you know that an APPLE is a HEALTHY snack?

UNSCRAMBLE THE WORD

Can you figure out what the following words are?

KDIRN TWEAR

TBLVEEAGE

PLEES ELLW

TRSSYBIYILONPE

AAIONTVC

FRUITS and VEGETABLES are HEALTHY and delicious!

WORD MIX UP

How many words can you make using the letters from the word

HEALTHY HABITS ?

Good hygiene – BRUSHING your teeth keeps them CLEAN and HEALTHY and that's a very HEALTHY HABIT!

DRAW IT

Reading is a VERY good habit!
Draw a picture of your favorite book.

Good hygiene – taking a BATH is great way way to keep your skin and hair CLEAN and HEALTHY.

MIX & MATCH

Match the pictures of Rock.

EXERCISING every day is important. Rock and Rambee Boo stretch before they go outside to play.

CONNECT THE DOTS

Help Rock find his boots by connecting the dots.

Did you know that SLEEPING is a HEALTHY HABIT?
It's important to get plenty of REST every night.

UNSCRAMBLE THE WORD

Can you figure out what the following words are?

RTA SSPPUIEL

SUEXEC EM

NAGEDIR

TCYTAVII

LIROOBCC

READING is a HEALTHY HABIT.
Reading helps your mind GROW.

COUNT WITH RAMBEE BOO

Count with Rambee Boo. How many ice cream cones can you count?

Rock likes to finish his HOMEWORK as soon as he comes home from school.

WORD MIX UP

How many words can you make using the letters from the word

SHOW KINDNESS ?

Rock and Rambee Boo practice PATIENCE by WAITING in line for their turn.

THINK OUTSIDE THE BOX

This is not AN ICE CREAM CONE. Finish the picture.

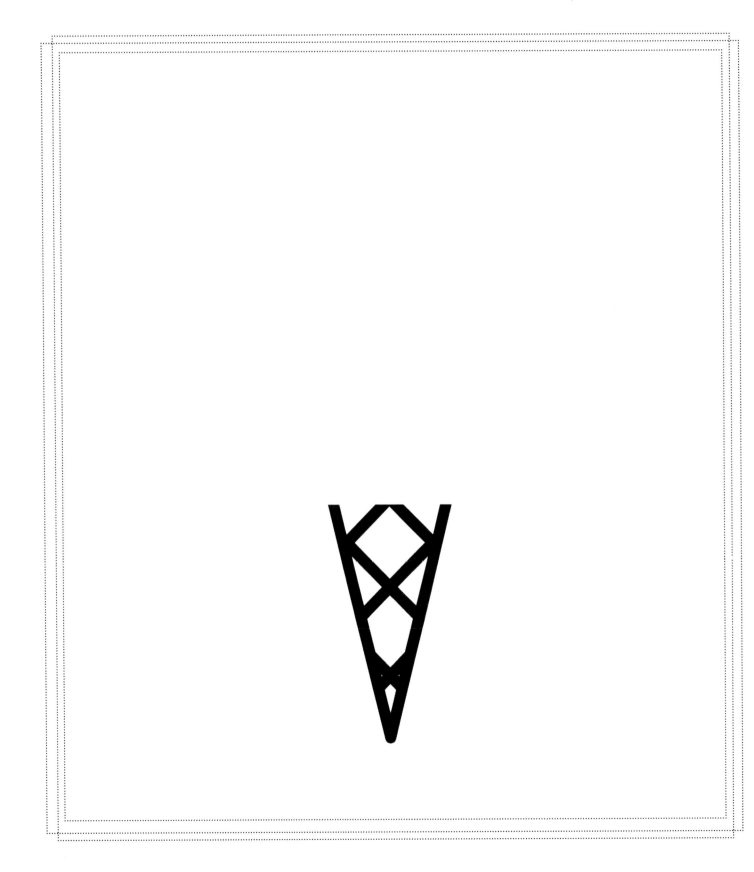

Design your own sock.

MIX & MATCH
Match the words showing good MANNERS.

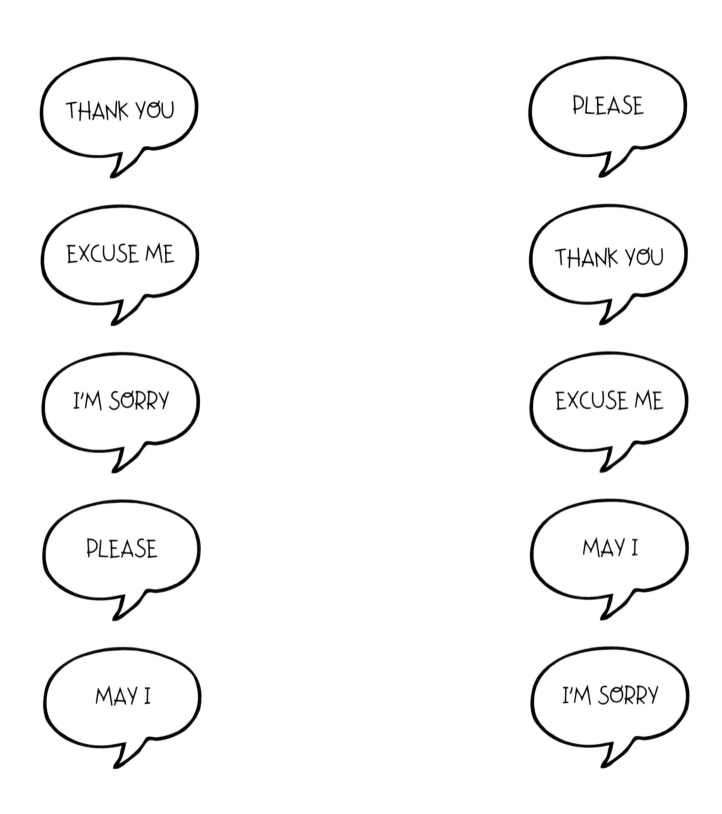

Rock and Rambee Boo LOVE each other!